BREAKFAST & BRUNCH

PUBLICATIONS INTERNATIONAL, LTD.

Photography: Burke Triolo Productions, Culver City, CA

Pictured on the front cover: Blueberry-Cheese Pancakes *(page 66)*.

Pictured on the back cover *(clockwise from top left):* Strawberry-Peach Cooler and Sparkling Apple Punch *(page 88),* Three-Egg Omelet *(page 8)* and Chocolate Waffles with Raspberry Syrup *(page 60).*

ISBN: 0-7853-1909-3

Manufactured in U.S.A.

8 7 6 5 4 3 2 1

Microwave ovens vary in wattage. The microwave cooking times given in this publication are approximate. Use the cooking times as guidelines and check for doneness before adding more time. Consult manufacturer's instructions for suitable microwave-safe cooking dishes.

BREAKFAST & BRUNCH

BREAKFAST BASICS

Start your day off right with a great breakfast. Included here are the basics to get you going—eggs, cereal, pancakes and waffles. They're all simple and easy to make, but tasty enough to capture your attention.

Pictured here is Three-Egg Omelet; see page 8 for recipe.

THREE-EGG OMELET

This omelet can be served plain or filled with one or more of the suggested fillings.

1 tablespoon butter or margarine
3 eggs, lightly beaten
    Salt and freshly ground pepper to taste
    Fillings (see below)

1. Melt butter in 10-inch skillet over medium heat.

2. Add eggs; lift cooked edges with spatula to allow uncooked eggs to flow under cooked portion. Season with salt and pepper. Shake pan to loosen omelet. Cook until set. Place desired fillings on ½ of omelet. Fold in half. Turn out onto plate.   *Makes 1 serving*

Filling Suggestions:

Shredded cheese
Chopped ham
Shredded crabmeat
Cooked small shrimp
Shredded cooked chicken
Cooked chopped bell pepper

Cooked sliced mushrooms
Chopped tomatoes
Cooked chopped onion
Cooked chopped asparagus,
    broccoli or other vegetables
Avocado slices

BERRY CRÊPES WITH ORANGE SAUCE

1 cup fresh blueberries
1 cup sliced strawberries
1 tablespoon sugar
3 packages (3 ounces each) cream cheese, softened
¼ cup honey
¾ cup orange juice
8 (6½-inch) Crêpes (page 9)

1. Combine blueberries, strawberries and sugar in small bowl; set aside.

2. To prepare sauce, beat cream cheese and honey until light; slowly beat in orange juice.

3. Spoon about ½ cup of berry filling in center of 1 crêpe. Spoon about 1 tablespoon sauce over berries. Roll up; place on serving plate. Repeat with remaining crêpes.

4. Pour remaining sauce over crêpes.   *Makes 4 servings*

CRÊPES

3/4 **cup all-purpose flour**
3 **eggs**
1 **cup milk**
3 **tablespoons butter or margarine, melted**
1/2 **teaspoon salt**
    About 2 tablespoons vegetable oil

1. Combine all ingredients except oil in blender or food processor container. Cover; process until combined. Cover and refrigerate at least 1 hour.

2. Brush 7-inch skillet with oil. Place over medium heat until hot. Add 3 tablespoons crêpe batter, tilting skillet to cover bottom evenly.

3. Cook until golden brown on bottom; turn over. Cook until browned on underside.

4. Stack crêpes between waxed paper squares to prevent sticking together. Repeat with remaining batter, oiling skillet occasionally.

Makes 16 crêpes

Tip: *Stacked crêpes can be placed in plastic bag and refrigerated 2 to 3 days or frozen up to 1 month. Thaw before using.*

SAUSAGE GRAVY

Serve over hot biscuits for a Southern-style breakfast.

1/4 **pound spicy bulk sausage**
1/4 **cup all-purpose flour**
2 **cups milk**
1/2 **teaspoon salt**
1/4 **teaspoon freshly ground pepper**

1. Cook sausage in medium saucepan over medium heat until browned, stirring to crumble.

2. Drain off all fat except about 2 tablespoons. Stir in flour. Cook, stirring constantly, until thickened and bubbly.

3. Gradually whisk in milk, salt and pepper. Cook, stirring constantly, until thickened and bubbly, about 5 minutes.

Makes about 4 servings

WAFFLES

Tightly wrap and freeze leftover waffles. They can go straight from the freezer to the toaster to make a quick hot breakfast!

2¼ cups all-purpose flour
2 tablespoons sugar
1 tablespoon baking powder
½ teaspoon salt
2 eggs, beaten
¼ cup vegetable oil
2 cups milk

1. Preheat waffle iron; grease lightly.

2. Sift flour, sugar, baking powder and salt into large bowl. Combine eggs, oil and milk in medium bowl. Stir liquid ingredients into dry ingredients until moistened.

3. For each waffle, pour about ¾ cup of batter into waffle iron. Close lid and bake until steaming stops.*   *Makes about 6 round waffles*

*Check the manufacturer's directions for recommended amount of batter and baking time.

STRAWBERRY SAUCE

Enjoy the fresh sweet taste of strawberries in the morning by serving this sauce with yogurt, hot cereal, pancakes or waffles.

1 pint strawberries, hulled
2 to 3 tablespoons sugar
1 tablespoon strawberry- or orange-flavored
    liqueur (optional)

Combine strawberries, sugar and liqueur in blender or food processor container. Cover; process until strawberries are puréed.

Makes 1½ cups

For crispier waffles, use less batter and let them cook for a few seconds longer after the steaming has stopped.

Waffles with Strawberry Sauce

POTATO-CARROT PANCAKES

1 pound russet potatoes, peeled
1 medium carrot, peeled
2 tablespoons minced green onion
1 tablespoon all-purpose flour
1 egg, beaten
½ teaspoon salt
⅛ teaspoon freshly ground pepper
2 tablespoons vegetable oil

1. Shred potatoes and carrot into medium bowl. Squeeze out excess moisture.

2. Add green onion, flour, egg, salt and pepper; mix well.

3. Heat oil in large skillet over medium heat. Drop spoonfuls of potato mixture into skillet; flatten to form thin circles.

4. Cook until browned on bottom; turn and cook until potatoes are tender, about 10 minutes total cooking time.

Makes about 12 pancakes

HASH-STUFFED POTATOES

4 large baking potatoes (10 to 12 ounces each)
1 can (15 ounces) corned beef hash
4 eggs

1. Preheat oven to 350°F.

2. Cut thin slice from top of each potato. Using melon baller, scoop out insides of each potato, leaving a ½-inch-thick wall. Fill each potato with about ½ cup of corned beef hash.

3. Place filled potatoes on lightly greased baking sheet. Bake 55 minutes or until tender when pierced with fork.

4. Prepare eggs as desired. Arrange on top of potatoes.

Makes 4 servings

Potato-Carrot Pancakes

DATE-NUT GRANOLA

The barley flakes add a nutty flavor. They can be purchased in some supermarkets and natural food stores. Use additional rolled oats if barley flakes are not available.

> 2 cups rolled oats
> 2 cups barley flakes
> 1 cup sliced almonds
> 1/3 cup vegetable oil
> 1/3 cup honey
> 1 teaspoon vanilla extract
> 1 cup chopped dates

1. Preheat oven to 350°F. Grease 13×9-inch baking pan.

2. Combine oats, barley flakes and almonds in large bowl; set aside.

3. Combine oil, honey and vanilla in small bowl. Pour honey mixture over oat mixture; stir well. Pour into prepared pan.

4. Bake about 25 minutes or until toasted, stirring frequently after the first 10 minutes. Stir in dates while mixture is still hot. Cool. Store tightly covered. *Makes 6 cups*

HOT CHOCOLATE

> 3 ounces semisweet chocolate, finely chopped
> 1/4 to 1/2 cup sugar
> 4 cups milk, divided
> 1 teaspoon vanilla extract
> Whipped cream or marshmallows (optional)

1. Combine chocolate, sugar and 1/4 cup milk in medium saucepan over medium-low heat. Cook, stirring constantly, until chocolate melts. Add remaining 3¾ cups milk; heat until hot, stirring occasionally. *Do not boil.* Stir in vanilla.

2. Beat with whisk until frothy. Pour into mugs and top with whipped cream or marshmallows, if desired. *Makes 4 servings*

Hot Cocoa: Substitute 1/4 cup unsweetened cocoa powder for semisweet chocolate and use 1/2 cup sugar; heat as above.

Hot Mocha: Add 4 teaspoons instant coffee to milk mixture; heat as above.

*Date-Nut Granola with
Summer Berries (page 16)*

PUFF PANCAKE WITH SUMMER BERRIES

2 eggs
½ cup all-purpose flour
½ cup milk
2 tablespoons butter or margarine, melted
1 tablespoon sugar
¼ teaspoon salt
Summer Berries (recipe follows)

1. Preheat oven to 425°F. Grease 10-inch ovenproof skillet.

2. With electric mixer, beat eggs. Add flour, milk, butter, sugar and salt; beat until smooth.

3. Pour batter into prepared skillet. Bake 15 minutes.

4. *Reduce oven temperature to 350°F.* Continue baking 10 to 15 minutes or until puffed and golden brown.

5. Serve pancake in skillet with Summer Berries.   *Makes 6 servings*

Summer Berries

2 cups blueberries
1 cup sliced strawberries
1 cup raspberries
Sugar to taste
Cream (optional)

Combine blueberries, strawberries and raspberries in medium bowl. Gently toss with sugar. Let stand 5 minutes. Top with cream if desired.

BAKING POWDER BISCUITS

2 cups all-purpose flour
1 tablespoon baking powder
½ teaspoon salt
¼ cup butter or margarine
3 tablespoons shortening
About ¾ cup milk

1. Preheat oven to 450°F. Grease baking sheet.

2. Sift flour, baking powder and salt into medium bowl. Using pastry blender or 2 knives, cut in butter and shortening until mixture resembles coarse crumbs. Stir in enough milk to make soft dough.

3. Turn out onto lightly floured surface. Knead dough lightly. Roll out ½ inch thick. Cut biscuit rounds with 2-inch cutter. Place on greased baking sheet.

4. Bake 8 to 10 minutes or until browned.   *Makes 16 biscuits*

Drop Biscuits: Make dough as above, increasing milk to about 1 cup or enough to make stiff batter. Drop by tablespoonfuls onto greased baking sheet. Bake 5 to 8 minutes or until browned.

Makes about 28 biscuits

CREAMY OATMEAL

Even when made with low-fat milk, this cooking method gives a rich, creamy flavor.

1⅓ **cups old-fashioned rolled oats**
3 **cups milk**
½ **cup raisins**
4 **teaspoons sugar**
⅛ **teaspoon salt**

1. Combine oats, milk, raisins, sugar and salt in medium saucepan over medium heat.

2. Bring to a boil, stirring occasionally. Reduce heat and simmer 5 minutes. Cover; remove from heat. Let stand 5 minutes.

Makes 4 servings

For a quick, make-ahead breakfast, freeze oatmeal in individual portions. It can be reheated quickly in the microwave, saving the fuss of measuring, cooking and cleaning up.

SUNRISE PANCAKES

Drizzle rich Vanilla Cream Syrup over these light, fluffy pancakes for a breakfast or brunch treat.

Vanilla Cream Syrup (recipe follows)
1 cup all-purpose flour
2 tablespoons sugar
1 teaspoon baking powder
1/2 teaspoon baking soda
1/2 teaspoon salt
2 eggs, slightly beaten
1/2 cup plain yogurt
1/2 cup water
2 tablespoons butter or margarine, melted

1. Prepare Vanilla Cream Syrup; set aside.

2. Combine flour, sugar, baking powder, baking soda and salt in large bowl.

3. Combine eggs, yogurt and water in medium bowl. Whisk in butter. Pour liquid ingredients, all at once, into dry ingredients; stir until moistened.

4. Preheat griddle or large skillet over medium heat; grease lightly. Pour about 1/4 cup batter onto hot griddle for each pancake; spread batter out to make 5-inch circles. Cook until tops of pancakes are bubbly and appear dry; turn and cook until browned, about 2 minutes.

Makes about 8 pancakes

Vanilla Cream Syrup

1/2 cup sugar
1/2 cup light corn syrup
1/2 cup whipping cream
1 teaspoon vanilla
1 nectarine, diced

Combine sugar, corn syrup and cream in 1-quart pan. Cook, stirring constantly, over medium heat until sugar is dissolved. Simmer 2 minutes or until syrup thickens slightly. Remove from heat. Stir in vanilla and nectarine.

Makes 1 cup

Sunrise Pancakes

BAKED EGGS

4 eggs
4 teaspoons milk
Salt and freshly ground pepper to taste

1. Preheat oven to 375°F. Grease 4 small baking dishes or custard cups.

2. Break 1 egg into each dish. Add 1 teaspoon of milk to each dish. Season with salt and pepper.

3. Bake about 15 minutes or until set.   *Makes 4 servings*

Baked Egg Options

Top eggs with desired amount of one or more of the following before baking; continue as above.

Light cream	*Chopped ham*
Salsa	*Minced chives*
Shredded cheese	*Minced fresh herbs*

POPOVERS

In just minutes you can make the batter for these crispy Popovers. They "pop" because the high ratio of liquid creates steam inside the little breads during baking.

3 eggs
1 cup milk
1 tablespoon butter or margarine, melted
1 cup all-purpose flour
1/4 teaspoon salt

1. Preheat oven to 375°F. Grease 12 muffin cups or 6 custard cups.

2. Beat eggs, milk and butter in medium bowl. Add flour and salt; beat until smooth.

3. Pour batter into prepared cups, filling about 3/4 full. (If using custard cups, place on baking sheet.) Bake 45 to 50 minutes or until brown and crispy. Serve immediately.   *Makes 12 small or 6 large popovers*

Cheese Popovers: Add 1/8 teaspoon garlic powder and 1/4 cup grated Parmesan cheese to batter. Bake as above.

SCRAMBLED EGGS

For great scrambled eggs, be sure to cook them slowly over medium heat. Do not overcook or they will become tough.

1 tablespoon butter or margarine
6 eggs, lightly beaten
1/2 teaspoon salt
1/4 teaspoon freshly ground pepper

1. Melt butter in 10-inch skillet over medium heat.

2. Season eggs with salt and pepper. Add eggs to skillet; cook, stirring gently and lifting to allow uncooked eggs to flow under cooked portion. Do not overcook; eggs should be soft with no liquid remaining.

Makes 4 servings

Scrambled Egg Options

Add one or more of the following to the beaten egg mixture and cook as above:

Chopped fresh herbs
Diced green chilies
Cooked chopped onions
Chopped sun-dried tomatoes
Cooked chopped vegetables

Shredded cheese
Crumbled cooked bacon or cooked sausage
Chopped smoked salmon
Chopped ham or Canadian bacon

BUTTERMILK PANCAKES

2 cups all-purpose flour
1 tablespoon sugar
1 1/2 teaspoons baking powder
1/2 teaspoon baking soda
1/2 teaspoon salt
1 egg, beaten
1 1/2 cups buttermilk
1/4 cup vegetable oil

1. Sift flour, sugar, baking powder, baking soda and salt into large bowl.

2. Combine egg, buttermilk and oil in medium bowl. Stir liquid ingredients into dry ingredients until moistened.

3. Preheat griddle or large skillet over medium heat; grease lightly. Pour about ½ cup batter onto hot griddle for each pancake. Cook until tops of pancakes are bubbly and appear dry; turn and cook until browned, about 2 minutes.   *Makes about 12 (5-inch) pancakes*

Silver Dollar Pancakes: Use 1 tablespoon batter for each pancake. Cook as above. Makes about 40 pancakes.

Buttermilk Substitution

If you don't have buttermilk on hand, try this easy substitution:

Place 1 tablespoon vinegar in measuring cup. Add milk to measure 1½ cups. Stir well; let stand 5 minutes.

COUNTRY BREAKFAST SAUSAGE

Sausage is surprisingly easy to make and is leaner than the commercial variety. Feel free to adjust the seasonings to your personal taste.

> 1 pound ground pork
> 1 teaspoon ground cumin
> ½ teaspoon dried leaf thyme
> ½ teaspoon dried leaf sage
> 1 teaspoon salt
> ½ teaspoon freshly ground pepper
> ⅛ teaspoon ground red (cayenne) pepper (optional)

1. Combine all ingredients in medium bowl; mix well. Cover and refrigerate overnight for flavors to blend.

2. Shape into 6 patties. Cook in lightly greased skillet over medium heat about 15 minutes or until browned on both sides and centers are no longer pink, turning occasionally.   *Makes 6 servings*

QUICK BREAKFASTS

No time for breakfast? There's no excuse with these terrific, quick-as-a-flash recipes. Make up one of the creamy Bagel Toppers or the Cereal Trail Mix the night before and you can be off and running the next morning with breakfast in hand.

Pictured here is Pita in the Morning; see page 26 for recipe.

PITA IN THE MORNING

    1 teaspoon butter or margarine
    2 eggs, lightly beaten
    1/4 teaspoon salt
      Dash pepper
    1 whole-wheat pita bread, cut in half
    1/4 cup sprouts
    2 tablespoons shredded Cheddar cheese
    2 tablespoons chopped tomato
      Avocado slices (optional)

1. Melt butter at HIGH (100%) 30 seconds in microwave-safe 1-quart casserole.

2. Season eggs with salt and pepper. Add eggs to casserole. Microwave at HIGH 1½ to 2½ minutes, stirring once. Do not overcook; eggs should be soft with no liquid remaining.

3. Open pita to make pockets. Arrange sprouts in pockets. Divide cheese and eggs evenly between pockets. Top with tomato and avocado slices.

Makes 1 sandwich

SUNRISE BURRITO

    2 ounces bulk sausage
    1/4 cup chopped onion
    2 eggs
    1 tablespoon water
    2 tablespoons canned chopped green chilies
    1 (10-inch) flour tortilla

1. Combine sausage and onion in microwave-safe 1-quart casserole. Microwave at HIGH (100%) 1½ to 2½ minutes or until sausage is brown and onion is tender, stirring once to break up meat.

2. Beat eggs with water in small bowl. Stir in chilies.

3. Drain fat from casserole. Add egg mixture to sausage and onion; mix well. Microwave at HIGH 1½ to 2½ minutes, stirring once. Do not overcook; eggs should be soft with no liquid remaining.

4. Microwave tortilla at HIGH about 15 seconds. Fill with scrambled egg mixture.

Makes 1 burrito

DANISH BAGEL

     1 raisin or blueberry bagel, halved
     ½ cup ricotta cheese
     8 teaspoons Cinnamon Sugar (recipe follows), divided
     1 peach, thinly sliced

1. Preheat broiler.

2. Spread bagel halves with ricotta. Sprinkle each bagel with 2 teaspoons Cinnamon Sugar. Arrange peach slices over cheese. Sprinkle with remaining Cinnamon Sugar.

3. Place bagel halves on baking sheet. Broil 6 inches from heat, about 4 minutes, until sugar is bubbly and mixture is hot. Serve warm.

Makes 2 servings

Cinnamon Sugar: Combine ½ cup sugar with 1 tablespoon ground cinnamon. Store in shaker-top jar.

MICROWAVED OATS CEREAL

     1¾ cups water
     ⅓ cup old-fashioned rolled oats
     ⅓ cup oat bran
     1 tablespoon brown sugar
     ¼ teaspoon ground cinnamon
     ⅛ teaspoon salt

1. Combine all ingredients in large microwave-safe bowl (cereal expands rapidly when it cooks). Cover with plastic wrap; vent.

2. Microwave on HIGH (100%) about 6 minutes or until thickened. Stir well. Let stand 2 minutes before serving.

Makes 2 servings

> *Add some excitement to your oatmeal by stirring in peanut butter, mashed bananas or molasses. (Or maybe all three!)*

BAGEL TOPPERS

All of these versatile spreads and toppers can be made ahead of time and kept on hand for a quick breakfast anytime.

Orange-Cream Bagel Spread

1 package (8 ounces) cream cheese, softened
3 tablespoons orange marmalade

Combine cream cheese and marmalade in small bowl.

Makes about 1 cup

Chocolate-Cream Bagel Spread

1 package (8 ounces) cream cheese, softened
3 ounces white chocolate, melted
2 tablespoons mini chocolate chips

Combine cream cheese and white chocolate in small bowl. Stir in chocolate chips.

Makes about 1¼ cups

Crab Bagel Spread

4 ounces cream cheese, softened
2 ounces crabmeat, shredded
4 teaspoons lemon juice
2 tablespoons chopped green onion tops
1 tablespoon milk

Combine all ingredients in medium bowl.

Makes about ¾ cup

Peanut Butter Topper

2 tablespoons creamy peanut butter
1 tablespoon raisins
1 small banana, thinly sliced
1 tablespoon sunflower kernels

Spread bagel with peanut butter. Top with raisins, banana slices and sunflower kernels.

Makes 1 to 2 servings

Crab Bagel Spread and
Peanut Butter Topper

TROPICAL TURKEY MELT

1 English muffin, split
1 teaspoon Dijon-style mustard
3 ounces smoked turkey slices
3 thin slices papaya
1 slice Monterey Jack cheese
Butter or margarine, softened

1. Spread inside of muffin halves with mustard. On 1 half, layer turkey, papaya and cheese. Press remaining muffin half, mustard-side-down, over cheese.

2. Spread butter on outsides of muffin halves.

3. Cook sandwich in small skillet over medium heat until toasted, about 4 minutes; turn and cook on remaining side until toasted and cheese is melted. Serve hot. *Makes 1 serving*

CEREAL TRAIL MIX

For a true breakfast-on-the-run, just take a bag of this mix, grab some milk and you've got a meal!

1/4 cup butter or margarine
2 tablespoons sugar
1 teaspoon ground cinnamon
1 cup bite-sized oat cereal squares
1 cup bite-sized wheat cereal squares
1 cup bite-sized rice cereal squares
1/4 cup toasted slivered almonds
3/4 cup raisins

1. Melt margarine at HIGH (100%) 1 1/2 minutes in large microwave-safe bowl. Add sugar and cinnamon; mix well. Add cereals and nuts; stir to coat.

2. Microwave at HIGH 2 minutes. Stir well. Microwave 2 minutes more; stir well. Add raisins. Microwave an additional 2 to 3 minutes, stirring well after 2 minutes. Spread on paper towels; mix will become crisp as it cools. Store tightly covered. *Makes about 4 cups*

Tropical Turkey Melt

BREAKFAST
IN A GLASS

Cool and refreshing, these shakes, smoothies and coolers are a great way to start the day. Just mix everything together in a blender, pour it into a glass and you are off and running!

Peachy Banana Shake

1 cup milk
$\frac{1}{2}$ cup vanilla ice cream
1 ripe banana, cut into chunks
1 peach, sliced
1 teaspoon vanilla extract

Place all ingredients in blender container. Cover; process until smooth.

Makes about 2 cups

Berry-Banana Breakfast Smoothie

1 carton (8 ounces) berry-flavored yogurt
1 ripe banana, cut into chunks
$\frac{1}{2}$ cup milk

Place all ingredients in blender container. Cover; process until smooth.

Makes about 2 cups

Peanut Butter-Banana Shake

1 ripe banana, cut into chunks
2 tablespoons peanut butter
$\frac{1}{2}$ cup vanilla ice cream
1 cup milk

Place all ingredients in blender container. Cover; process until smooth.

Makes about 2 cups

Mocha Cooler

1 cup milk
1 tablespoon instant coffee granules
1 tablespoon chocolate syrup
$\frac{1}{4}$ cup vanilla or coffee ice cream

Place all ingredients in blender container. Cover; process until smooth.

Makes about $1\frac{1}{2}$ cups

Rise 'n' Shine Shake

1 cup milk
1 cup strawberries, hulled
1 kiwifruit, peeled and quartered
1/4 cup vanilla or strawberry frozen yogurt
1 to 2 tablespoons sugar

Place all ingredients in blender container. Cover; process until smooth.

Makes about 1 1/2 cups

Raspberry Lemon Smoothie

1 cup frozen raspberries
1 carton (8 ounces) lemon-flavored yogurt
1/2 cup milk
1 teaspoon vanilla

Place all ingredients in blender container. Cover; process until smooth.

Makes about 1 1/2 cups

Mango Yogurt Drink

1/2 cup plain yogurt
1 ripe mango, peeled, seeded and sliced
1/4 cup orange juice
1 teaspoon honey
2 ice cubes
   Milk (optional)

Place all ingredients in blender container. Cover; process until smooth.
Add milk to obtain preferred consistency. *Makes about 1 1/2 cups*

Tip: *The skin of most mangos tinges with more red or yellow as the fruit ripens. Mangos are ready to eat when they yield to gentle pressure.*

A Nutritious Breakfast

Nutritionists suggest you include foods from three of the four food groups for a healthy breakfast. The four food groups are: milk and dairy products, fruits and vegetables, breads and cereals and meat and protein foods (including eggs and dried peas and beans).

BREAKFAST PARFAIT

½ cup Date-Nut Granola (page 14) or your favorite
    granola
¼ cup plain nonfat yogurt or cottage cheese
½ cup sliced strawberries
½ ripe banana, sliced

Place half of granola in parfait glass or glass bowl. Top with half of yogurt. Arrange half of strawberries and the banana over yogurt. Top with remaining granola, yogurt and strawberries.   *Makes 1 serving*

DELUXE TURKEY PITA MELT

1 whole-wheat pita bread
2 ounces Brie or other soft cheese
2 ounces sliced smoked turkey
1 medium tomato, thinly sliced
¼ teaspoon dried leaf basil
    Alfalfa sprouts or shredded lettuce

1. Preheat oven to 400°F. Cut pita around edge to make 2 flat pieces.

2. Spread inside of each pita half with Brie. Top with turkey, tomato and basil.

3. Place pita halves on baking sheet. Bake about 5 minutes or until cheese melts and topping is hot.

4. Remove from oven; top with alfalfa sprouts. Serve warm.
Makes 2 servings

Vitamin C

The morning meal is a good time to get your daily dose of vitamin C. Good sources include orange, grapefruit and tomato juices and strawberries, cantaloupe and kiwifruit.

EGG ENTRÉES

No breakfast or brunch would be complete without eggs, and this delightful chapter presents them in all their glory. From classic dishes such as quiches and omelets to unique creations like Ham & Cheese Grits Soufflé and Breakfast in a Loaf, there's a recipe here to fit every menu.

Pictured here are Egg Blossoms; see page 38 for recipe, with Papaya-Kiwifruit Salad with Orange Dressing; see page 86 for recipe.

EGG BLOSSOMS

Egg Blossoms will add a bright and cheery note to your morning meal.

> 4 sheets filo pastry
> 2 tablespoons butter, melted
> 4 teaspoons grated Parmesan cheese
> 4 eggs
> 4 teaspoons minced green onion
>   Salt and freshly ground pepper
>   Tomato Sauce (recipe follows)

1. Preheat oven to 350°F. Grease 4 (2½-inch) muffin cups.

2. Brush 1 sheet of filo with butter. Top with another sheet; brush with butter. Cut stack into 6 (4-inch) squares. Repeat with remaining 2 sheets. Stack 3 squares together, rotating so corners do not overlap. Press into greased muffin cup. Repeat with remaining squares.

3. Sprinkle 1 teaspoon cheese into each filo-lined cup. Break 1 egg into each cup. Sprinkle onion over eggs. Season with salt and pepper. Bake 15 to 20 minutes or until pastry is golden and eggs are set. Serve with Tomato Sauce.

Makes 4 servings

Tomato Sauce

> 1 can (16 ounces) whole tomatoes, undrained, chopped
> 1 clove garlic, minced
> ½ cup chopped onion
> 1 tablespoon white wine vinegar
> ¼ teaspoon dried leaf oregano
> ½ teaspoon salt

Combine tomatoes, garlic, onion, vinegar, oregano and salt in medium saucepan. Cook, stirring occasionally, over medium heat until onion is tender, about 20 minutes. Serve warm.

CHILIES RELLENOS CASSEROLE

For a weekend brunch, bake this in individual baking dishes, then lavish with your choice of garnishes.

3 eggs, separated
3/4 cup milk
3/4 cup all-purpose flour
1/2 teaspoon salt
1 tablespoon butter or margarine
1/2 cup chopped onion
2 cans (7 ounces each) whole green chilies, drained
8 slices (1 ounce each) Monterey Jack cheese, cut into halves
Garnishes: Sour cream, sliced green onions, pitted ripe olive slices, guacamole and salsa

1. Preheat oven to 350°F.

2. Combine egg yolks, milk, flour and salt in blender or food processor container. Cover; process until smooth. Pour into bowl and let stand.

3. Melt butter in small skillet over medium heat. Add onion; cook until tender.

4. Pat chilies dry with paper towels. Slit each chili lengthwise and carefully remove seeds. Place 2 halves of cheese and 1 tablespoon onion in each chili; reshape chilies to cover cheese.

5. Place chilies in single layer in greased 13×9-inch baking dish.

6. In small clean bowl, beat egg whites until soft peaks form; fold into yolk mixture. Pour over chilies.

7. Bake 20 to 25 minutes or until topping is puffed and knife inserted in center comes out clean. Broil 4 inches below heat 30 seconds or until topping is golden brown. Serve with desired garnishes.

Makes 4 servings

BREAKFAST
IN A LOAF

    1 round loaf bread (8 to 9 inches)
    4 ounces sliced ham
  1/2 red bell pepper, thinly sliced crosswise
  1/2 cup (2 ounces) shredded Monterey Jack cheese
  1/2 cup (2 ounces) shredded Cheddar cheese
    1 recipe Scrambled Eggs (page 22)
  1/2 cup sliced ripe olives
    1 medium tomato, thinly sliced
    8 ounces mushrooms, sliced, cooked

1. Preheat oven to 350°F. Cut 2-inch slice from top of loaf; set aside for lid. Remove soft interior of loaf, leaving a 1-inch-thick wall and bottom.

2. Place ham in bottom of loaf. Top with bell pepper rings; sprinkle with half of cheeses. Layer Scrambled Eggs, olives and tomato over cheeses. Top with remaining cheeses and mushrooms.

3. Place lid on loaf. Wrap in foil. Place on baking sheet. Bake about 30 minutes or until heated through. Cut into 8 wedges.

Makes 8 servings

HAM & CHEESE
GRITS SOUFFLÉ

    3 cups water
  3/4 cup quick-cooking grits
  1/2 teaspoon salt
  1/2 cup (2 ounces) shredded mozzarella cheese
    2 ounces ham, finely chopped
    2 tablespoons minced chives
    2 eggs, separated
      Dash hot pepper sauce

1. Preheat oven to 375°F. Grease 1½-quart soufflé dish or deep casserole.

2. Bring water to a boil in medium saucepan. Stir in grits and salt. Cook, stirring frequently, about 5 minutes or until thickened. Stir in cheese, ham, chives, egg yolks and hot pepper sauce.

3. In small clean bowl, beat egg whites until stiff but not dry; fold into grits mixture. Pour into prepared dish. Bake about 30 minutes or until puffed and golden. Serve immediately.

Makes 4 to 6 servings

Breakfast in a Loaf

MUSHROOM & ONION EGG BAKE

1 tablespoon vegetable oil
4 green onions, chopped
4 ounces mushrooms, sliced
1 cup low-fat cottage cheese
1 cup sour cream
6 eggs
2 tablespoons all-purpose flour
1/4 teaspoon salt
1/8 teaspoon freshly ground pepper
Dash hot pepper sauce

1. Preheat oven to 350°F. Grease shallow 1-quart baking dish.

2. Heat oil in medium skillet over medium heat. Add onions and mushrooms; cook until tender. Set aside.

3. In blender or food processor, process cottage cheese until almost smooth. Add sour cream, eggs, flour, salt, pepper and hot pepper sauce; process until combined. Stir in onions and mushrooms. Pour into greased dish. Bake about 40 minutes or until knife inserted near center comes out clean. *Makes about 6 servings*

STUFFED TOMATOES & CREAMED SPINACH

4 medium tomatoes
1/4 cup grated Parmesan cheese
4 eggs
4 teaspoons minced green onion
Salt and freshly ground pepper to taste
Creamed Spinach (page 44)

1. Preheat oven to 375°F.

2. Cut thin slice off blossom end of each tomato; remove seeds and pulp, being careful not to pierce side of tomato. Place tomato shells in shallow baking dish.

3. Sprinkle 1 tablespoon Parmesan cheese inside each tomato. Break an egg into each tomato. Top with onion, salt and pepper. Bake 15 to 20 minutes or until eggs are set. Serve with Creamed Spinach.
Makes 4 servings

Mushroom & Onion Egg Bake with
Country Breakfast Sausage (page 23)

Creamed Spinach

1 package (10 ounces) frozen chopped spinach,
    thawed
2 tablespoons butter or margarine
2 tablespoons all-purpose flour
1 cup milk
1/4 teaspoon salt
    Dash freshly ground pepper
1 tablespoon grated Parmesan cheese (optional)

1. Press spinach to remove all moisture; set aside. Melt butter in medium saucepan over medium heat. Stir in flour; cook until bubbly.

2. Slowly stir in milk. Cook until thickened. Add spinach; continue cooking over low heat, stirring constantly, about 5 minutes or until spinach is tender. Season with salt, pepper and cheese.

EASY CRAB-ASPARAGUS PIE

4 ounces crabmeat, shredded
12 ounces fresh asparagus, cooked
1/2 cup chopped onion, cooked
1 cup (4 ounces) shredded Monterey Jack cheese
1/4 cup grated Parmesan cheese
    Freshly ground pepper
3/4 cup all-purpose flour
3/4 teaspoon baking powder
1/2 teaspoon salt
2 tablespoons butter or margarine, chilled
1 1/2 cups milk
4 eggs

1. Preheat oven to 350°F. Lightly grease 10-inch quiche dish or pie plate.

2. Layer crabmeat, asparagus and onion in prepared pie plate. Top with cheeses. Season with pepper.

3. Combine flour, baking powder and salt in large bowl. With pastry blender or 2 knives, cut in butter. Add milk and eggs; stir until blended. Pour over vegetables and cheeses.

4. Bake about 30 minutes or until filling is puffed and knife inserted near center comes out clean. Serve hot.   *Makes 6 servings*

SPANISH POTATO OMELET

Cut this cook-ahead omelet into thin wedges to serve as an appetizer. It is sturdy enough to pick up with your fingers and is traditionally served at room temperature.

   1/4 **cup olive oil**
   1/4 **cup vegetable oil**
   1 **pound thin-skinned red or white potatoes, cut into**
       1/8-inch slices
   1/2 **teaspoon salt, divided**
   1 **small onion, cut in half lengthwise, thinly sliced**
       crosswise
   1/4 **cup chopped green bell pepper**
   1/4 **cup chopped red bell pepper**
   3 **eggs**

1. Heat oils in large skillet over medium-high heat. Add potatoes to hot oil. Turn with spatula several times to coat all slices with oil.

2. Sprinkle with 1/4 teaspoon salt. Cook 6 to 9 minutes or until potatoes become translucent, turning occasionally. Add onion and peppers. Reduce heat to medium.

3. Cook 10 minutes or until potatoes are tender, turning occasionally. Drain mixture in colander placed in large bowl; reserve oil. Let potato mixture stand until cool.

4. Beat eggs with remaining 1/4 teaspoon salt in large bowl. Gently stir in potato mixture; lightly press into bowl until mixture is covered with eggs. Let stand 15 minutes.

5. Heat 2 teaspoons reserved oil in 6-inch skillet over medium-high heat. Spread potato mixture in pan to form solid layer. Cook until egg on bottom and side of pan is set but top still looks moist.

6. Cover pan with plate. Flip omelet onto plate, then slide omelet back into pan uncooked side down. Continue to cook until bottom is lightly browned.

7. Slide omelet onto serving plate. Let stand 30 minutes before serving. Cut into 8 wedges to serve.   *Makes 8 servings*

EGGS RANCHEROS

Just like the cowboys eat, this flavorful breakfast will fill you up!

RANCHERO SAUCE
 1 can (16 ounces) whole tomatoes, undrained, chopped
 1 can (4 ounces) chopped green chilies, drained
 ½ cup chopped onion
 1 tablespoon white wine vinegar
 ¼ teaspoon salt

EGGS
 1 tablespoon vegetable oil
 4 eggs
   Salt and pepper to taste
 1 can (30 ounces) refried beans
 1 cup (4 ounces) shredded Cheddar cheese
 4 corn tortillas

1. For Ranchero Sauce, combine tomatoes, chilies, onion, vinegar and salt in medium saucepan. Cook, stirring occasionally, over medium heat until onion is tender, about 20 minutes. Keep warm.

2. For Eggs, heat oil in large skillet over medium-low heat. Break eggs into skillet. Season with salt and pepper. Cook 2 to 3 minutes or until eggs are set. Turn eggs for over-easy eggs.

3. Heat beans in medium saucepan. Spoon beans onto 4 warmed plates; sprinkle evenly with cheese.

4. Heat tortillas. Place 1 tortilla on each plate; top each tortilla with 1 egg. Spoon warm Ranchero Sauce over eggs. *Makes 4 servings*

Tip: *To heat tortillas in a conventional oven, wrap in foil and place in 350°F oven about 10 minutes. To heat tortillas in a microwave oven; wrap loosely in a damp paper towel. Heat on HIGH (100%) about 1 minute.*

Eggs Rancheros

ARTICHOKE
FRITTATA

*A frittata is an Italian omelet with the filling mixed in with the eggs
instead of folded inside.*

1 can (14 ounces) artichoke hearts, drained and rinsed
    Olive oil
½ cup minced green onions
5 eggs
½ cup (2 ounces) shredded Swiss cheese
2 tablespoons grated Parmesan cheese
1 tablespoon minced fresh savory *or* 1 teaspoon dried
    leaf savory
1 tablespoon minced fresh parsley
1 teaspoon salt
    Freshly ground pepper to taste

1. Chop artichoke hearts; set aside.

2. Heat 1 tablespoon olive oil in 10-inch skillet over medium heat. Add
green onions; cook until tender. Remove with slotted spoon; set aside.

3. Beat eggs in medium bowl until light. Stir in artichokes, green onions,
cheeses, herbs, salt and pepper.

4. Heat 1½ teaspoons olive oil in same skillet over medium heat. Pour
egg mixture into skillet.

5. Cook 4 to 5 minutes or until bottom is lightly browned. Place large
plate over skillet. Invert frittata onto plate. Return frittata, uncooked side
down, to skillet. Cook about 4 minutes more or until center is just set.
Cut into 6 wedges to serve.   *Makes 6 servings*

Cooking Eggs

*Remember when cooking eggs that too high a temperature
will cause them to be tough and rubbery. Use either low or
medium heat.*

---

*Artichoke Frittata with Greek Three
Pepper Salad (page 77)*

CALIFORNIA CROISSANTS

1 teaspoon vinegar*
4 eggs
2 croissants, halved and toasted
4 slices tomato
½ avocado, sliced crosswise
8 slices crisp-cooked bacon
Mornay Sauce (recipe follows)
Chopped chives and sprouts

1. Fill wide saucepan or deep skillet with about 1½ inches water. Add vinegar. Bring to a simmer. Break 1 egg into shallow cup or saucer. Gently slide egg into simmering water. Repeat with remaining eggs.

2. Cook eggs 3 to 4 minutes or until set. Carefully remove eggs with slotted spoon; drain on paper towels.

3. Place croissant half on each plate. Layer tomato, avocado and bacon on croissant. Top with poached eggs. Divide Mornay Sauce equally among croissants. Garnish with chives and sprouts.

Makes 4 servings

*Adding vinegar to the water helps keep the egg white intact while poaching.

Mornay Sauce

2 tablespoons butter or margarine
2 tablespoons all-purpose flour
1½ cups milk
¼ cup (1 ounce) shredded Cheddar cheese
2 tablespoons grated Parmesan cheese
½ teaspoon Dijon-style mustard
¼ teaspoon salt
⅛ teaspoon white pepper

1. Melt butter in medium saucepan over medium heat. Add flour; stir until bubbly.

2. Gradually stir in milk. Cook, stirring constantly, until mixture comes to a boil. Continue cooking until thickened.

3. Stir in cheeses, mustard, salt and pepper. Remove from heat and continue stirring until cheese melts.   *Makes about 1¾ cups*

California Croissant

SCRAMBLED EGGS
WITH TAMALES

 1 can (15 ounces) tamales
 8 eggs
 2 tablespoons milk
 ½ teaspoon salt
 2 tablespoons butter or margarine
 1 large tomato, chopped
 2 tablespoons minced onion
 2 tablespoons diced green chilies
 1 cup (4 ounces) shredded Monterey Jack cheese

1. Preheat oven to 350°F.

2. Drain tamales, reserving ½ of sauce from can. Remove paper wrappings from tamales; place tamales in single layer in 10×6-inch baking dish. Cover with reserved sauce. Bake 10 minutes or until heated through.

3. Whisk eggs, milk and salt in medium bowl. Set aside.

4. Melt butter in large skillet over medium heat. Add tomato, onion and chilies. Cook 2 minutes or until vegetables are heated through. Add egg mixture. Cook, stirring gently, until eggs are soft set.

5. Remove tamales from oven. Spoon eggs over tamales; sprinkle with cheese. Broil 4 inches below heat 30 seconds or just until cheese melts.

Makes 4 to 6 servings

FRESH STRAWBERRY
BANANA OMELETS

A fruit-filled omelet can be a refreshing change of pace.

 1 cup sliced strawberries
 1 banana, sliced
 4 teaspoons sugar
 ¼ teaspoon grated lemon peel
 1 tablespoon lemon juice
 4 eggs
 ¼ cup water
 ¼ teaspoon salt
 2 tablespoons butter or margarine, divided

1. Combine strawberries, banana, sugar, lemon peel and juice in medium bowl; mix lightly. Cover; let stand 15 minutes at room temperature.

2. Combine eggs, water and salt in small bowl. Melt 1 tablespoon butter in 8-inch omelet pan or skillet over medium heat.

3. Add ½ egg mixture (about ½ cup). Lift cooked edges with spatula to allow uncooked eggs to flow under cooked portion. Shake pan to loosen omelet.

4. Cook until almost set; add ½ cup fruit filling. Fold in half. Turn out onto plate. Keep warm. Repeat with remaining egg mixture. Top with remaining egg filling. *Makes 2 servings*

SPINACH CHEESE STRATA

This is a perfect make-ahead meal because it must be refrigerated for at least 6 hours. So make it up the day before, refrigerate overnight and just pop it in the oven about an hour before brunch.

6 slices whole wheat bread
2 tablespoons butter or margarine, softened
1 cup (4 ounces) shredded Cheddar cheese
½ cup (2 ounces) shredded Monterey Jack cheese
1¼ cups milk
6 eggs, lightly beaten
1 package (10 ounces) frozen spinach, thawed and well drained
¼ teaspoon salt
⅛ teaspoon pepper

1. Spread bread with butter. Arrange buttered slices in single layer in greased 13×9-inch baking dish. Sprinkle with cheeses.

2. Combine milk, eggs, spinach, salt and pepper in large bowl; stir well. Pour over bread and cheese.

3. Cover; refrigerate at least 6 hours or overnight.

4. Bake, uncovered, at 350°F about 1 hour or until puffy and lightly golden. *Makes 4 to 6 servings*

BREADS & COFFEECAKES

Syrup-drenched French toast, crispy waffles, fluffy pancakes and muffins and coffeecakes fresh from the oven—you'll love the variety of fantastic flavors when making these exceptional treats for your next breakfast or brunch.

Pictured here is French Raisin Toast; see page 56 for recipe.

FRENCH
RAISIN TOAST

2 tablespoons sugar
1 teaspoon ground cinnamon
4 eggs, lightly beaten
½ cup milk
8 slices raisin bread
4 tablespoons butter or margarine, divided
Powdered sugar

1. Combine sugar and cinnamon in wide shallow bowl. Beat in eggs and milk. Add bread; let stand to coat, then turn to coat other side.

2. Heat 2 tablespoons of butter in large skillet over medium-low heat. Add bread slices; cook until brown. Turn and cook other side. Remove and keep warm. Repeat with remaining butter and bread. Sprinkle with powdered sugar. *Makes 4 servings*

HAM & SWISS
CHEESE BISCUITS

This classy combination is terrific as a breakfast biscuit and any leftovers make great snacks.

2 cups all-purpose flour
2 teaspoons baking powder
½ teaspoon baking soda
½ cup butter or margarine, chilled, cut into pieces
½ cup (2 ounces) shredded Swiss cheese
2 ounces ham, minced
About ⅔ cup buttermilk

1. Preheat oven to 450°F. Grease baking sheet.

2. Sift flour, baking powder and baking soda into medium bowl. Using pastry blender or 2 knives, cut in butter until mixture resembles coarse crumbs. Stir in cheese, ham and enough buttermilk to make soft dough.

3. Turn out dough onto lightly floured surface; knead lightly. Roll out dough ½ inch thick. Cut biscuit rounds with 2-inch cutter. Place on greased baking sheet.

4. Bake about 10 minutes or until browned. *Makes about 18 biscuits*

PEAR BREAD PUDDING

          4 eggs, beaten
          3/4 cup sugar
          3 cups milk
          1 tablespoon vanilla extract
          8 slices egg bread, crusts removed
          3 to 4 tablespoons butter or margarine, softened
          1 can (16 ounces) sliced pears, drained, sliced *or* 1 cup
             sliced cooked pears
          Cream or Vanilla Sauce (recipe follows)

1. Grease 9×9-inch baking dish.

2. Combine eggs and sugar in large bowl. Gradually stir in milk and vanilla; set aside.

3. Lightly spread both sides of bread with butter. Arrange layer of bread slices in dish; top with another layer of bread slices. Arrange pear slices on bread. Pour egg mixture over bread and pears; let stand 30 minutes.

4. Preheat oven to 350°F. Place dish in larger pan, then fill larger pan with enough hot water to come halfway up sides of dish.

5. Bake about 55 minutes or until mixture is puffed and knife inserted near center comes out clean. Serve warm with cream or Vanilla Sauce.
Makes 10 servings

Vanilla Sauce

          1 cup sugar
          3 tablespoons all-purpose flour
          3 tablespoons cornstarch
       4 1/2 cups milk
          4 egg yolks, beaten
          2 tablespoons butter or margarine
          1 tablespoon vanilla extract

1. Combine sugar, flour and cornstarch in large saucepan.

2. Gradually whisk in milk. Cook over medium heat, stirring constantly, until mixture comes to a boil, 10 to 15 minutes. Remove from heat.

3. Stir 1 cup of hot mixture into egg yolks. Stir egg yolk mixture into hot mixture; return to heat. Cook, stirring constantly, until mixture is bubbly. Continue cooking, stirring constantly, 2 minutes. Pour into heatproof bowl; stir in butter and cool. Stir in vanilla. *Makes about 5 cups*

BLUEBERRY LATTICE COFFEECAKE

1 package (¼ ounce) active dry yeast
1 teaspoon sugar
¼ cup warm water (110°F)
1 egg, beaten
½ cup butter or margarine, softened
⅓ cup milk
3 cups all-purpose flour
¼ cup sugar
½ teaspoon salt
2 packages (8 ounces each) cream cheese, softened
2 egg yolks
⅔ cup sugar
1 teaspoon vanilla extract or lemon extract
1 tablespoon grated lemon peel (optional)
1 cup fresh or frozen blueberries

1. Dissolve yeast and 1 teaspoon sugar in warm water in large bowl. Let stand 10 minutes.

2. Beat in 1 egg, butter and milk. Beat in flour, ¼ cup sugar and salt to make soft dough. Knead on lightly floured surface about 10 minutes or until smooth and satiny, adding more flour as necessary to prevent sticking. Cover and let rest while making filling.

3. Combine cream cheese, 2 egg yolks, ⅔ cup sugar, vanilla and lemon peel in medium bowl. Beat until combined; set aside.

4. Grease 13×9-inch pan. Divide dough into thirds; set ⅓ aside. Roll out remaining ⅔ of dough to 13×9-inch rectangle. Place in greased pan and press dough ½ inch up sides to contain filling.

5. Spoon filling into dough-lined pan. Arrange blueberries over filling, pressing blueberries lightly into filling. Roll out remaining dough to 10-inch square. Cut dough into 1-inch strips. Arrange strips diagonally across pan in lattice pattern over filling, sealing strips to edges.

6. Cover with plastic wrap and refrigerate at least 2 hours or overnight.

7. Preheat oven to 350°F. Bake, uncovered, about 40 minutes or until lightly browned and filling is set. Serve warm or at room temperature.

Makes 1 coffeecake (15 servings)

Top: Pear Bread Pudding (page 57)
Bottom: Blueberry Lattice Coffeecake

CHOCOLATE WAFFLES

A fruity topping like Raspberry Syrup is the perfect complement to the delicate chocolate flavor of these waffles.

2 cups all-purpose flour
1/4 cup unsweetened cocoa powder
2 tablespoons sugar
1 tablespoon baking powder
1/2 teaspoon salt
2 cups milk
2 eggs, beaten
1/4 cup vegetable oil
1 teaspoon vanilla extract
Raspberry Syrup (recipe follows)

1. Preheat waffle iron; grease lightly.

2. Sift flour, cocoa, sugar, baking powder and salt into large bowl. Combine milk, eggs, oil and vanilla in small bowl. Stir liquid ingredients into dry ingredients until moistened.

3. For each waffle, pour about 3/4 cup batter into waffle iron. Close lid and bake until steaming stops.* Serve with Raspberry Syrup.

Makes about 6 waffles

*Check manufacturer's directions for recommended amount of batter and baking time.

Raspberry Syrup

1 cup water
1 cup sugar
1 package (10 ounces) frozen raspberries in syrup

1. Combine water and sugar in large saucepan. Cook over medium heat, stirring constantly, until sugar has dissolved. Continue cooking until mixture thickens slightly, about 10 minutes.

2. Stir in frozen raspberries; cook, stirring, until berries are thawed. Bring to a boil; continue cooking until syrup thickens slightly, about 5 to 10 minutes. Serve warm.

Makes about 1 1/3 cups

*Chocolate Waffles with
Raspberry Syrup*

STRAWBERRY MUFFINS

1¼ cups all-purpose flour
2½ teaspoons baking powder
½ teaspoon salt
1 cup rolled oats
½ cup sugar
1 cup milk
½ cup butter or margarine, melted
1 egg, beaten
1 teaspoon vanilla extract
1 cup chopped strawberries

1. Preheat oven to 425°F. Grease 12 (2½-inch) muffin cups.

2. Sift flour, baking powder and salt into large bowl. Stir in rolled oats and sugar; set aside. Combine milk, butter, egg and vanilla in small bowl. Stir milk mixture into dry ingredients just until moistened. Stir in strawberries.

3. Spoon batter into prepared muffin cups, filling each ⅔ full. Bake 15 to 18 minutes or until lightly browned and toothpick inserted in center comes out clean. *Makes 12 muffins*

CROISSANT TOAST

Although croissants make this dish extra special, the egg mixture can also be used with French bread, cinnamon bread or white bread.

4 eggs, lightly beaten
¾ cup milk
2 tablespoons brandy (optional)
1 tablespoon sugar
2 teaspoons vanilla extract
4 day-old croissants, halved horizontally
4 tablespoons butter or margarine, divided

1. Beat eggs, milk, brandy, sugar and vanilla in wide shallow bowl. Add croissants, cut-side down; let stand to coat, then turn to coat other side.

2. Heat 2 tablespoons butter in large skillet over medium-low heat. Add croissant halves; cook until brown. Turn and cook other side. Remove and keep warm. Repeat with remaining butter and croissants. Serve warm with syrup. *Makes 4 servings*

Strawberry Muffins with Apple-Almond Coffeecake (page 64)

APPLE-ALMOND
COFFEECAKES

You can prepare this coffeecake the night before, top it with the apples just before baking and have the aroma of fresh coffeecake filling the house when your guests arrive.

1 package (¼ ounce) active dry yeast
1 teaspoon sugar
¼ cup warm water (110°F)
4 eggs, divided
½ cup butter or margarine, softened
⅓ cup milk
3 cups all-purpose flour
1¼ cups sugar, divided
½ teaspoon salt
1½ packages (7 ounces each) almond paste
4 small apples

1. Dissolve yeast and 1 teaspoon sugar in warm water in large bowl. Let stand 5 minutes or until mixture is bubbly. (If yeast does not bubble, it is no longer active and dough will not rise.)

2. Beat in 1 egg, butter and milk. Beat in flour, ¼ cup sugar and salt to make soft dough. Knead on lightly floured surface about 10 minutes or until smooth and satiny, adding flour as necessary to prevent sticking. Cover and let rest while making filling.

3. Cut almond paste into small pieces. Combine almond paste, remaining 3 eggs and ¾ cup sugar in blender or food processor container. Cover; process until combined. Set aside.

4. Grease two 9-inch round cake pans. Divide dough in half. Roll out ½ of dough to 9-inch circle. Place in greased pan and press dough ½ inch up side to contain filling. Repeat with remaining dough.

5. Divide almond filling equally between pans. Cover with plastic wrap and refrigerate at least 2 hours or overnight.

6. Preheat oven to 350°F. Core apples and cut into thin slices; do not peel. Arrange apple slices over almond filling. Sprinkle each coffeecake with 2 tablespoons sugar. Bake 40 to 50 minutes or until filling is set. Serve warm or at room temperature.

Makes 2 coffeecakes (8 to 10 servings each)

APRICOT RING

FILLING
- 1 cup dried apricots, chopped
- 1 cup apple juice
- ³/₄ cup sugar or to taste

DOUGH
- 1 package (¹/₄ ounce) active dry yeast
- 4 tablespoons sugar, divided
- 1 cup warm water (110°F)
- About 4 cups all-purpose flour, divided
- 1 teaspoon salt
- 2 eggs, beaten
- ¹/₄ cup butter or margarine, softened
- 1 egg white, lightly beaten
- 2 tablespoons sliced almonds

1. To make filling, combine apricots and apple juice in small saucepan over medium heat. Cover and cook, stirring occasionally, about 12 minutes or until apricots are tender and juice is absorbed. Stir in sugar to taste. Cook, stirring constantly, about 3 minutes or until mixture is thick paste. Cool.

2. To make dough, dissolve yeast and 1 tablespoon sugar in warm water in large bowl of electric mixer. Let stand 10 minutes. Add remaining 3 tablespoons sugar, 1 cup flour and salt.

3. Beat with electric mixer 2 minutes. Add eggs and butter. Beat 1 minute. Stir in enough of remaining 3 cups flour to make soft dough.

4. Knead dough on lightly floured surface about 10 minutes or until smooth, adding flour as necessary to prevent sticking. Cover and let rest 20 minutes.

5. Grease large baking sheet. On lightly floured surface, roll dough to 18×11-inch rectangle. Spread filling over dough. Roll up jellyroll-style, starting at long side. Seal edge; form into ring on greased baking sheet, sealing ends.

6. Cut ring at 1-inch intervals about two-thirds of the way through, using kitchen scissors or sharp knife. Turn each slice outward to form a petal as you cut.

7. Cover with damp cloth and let rise in warm place until doubled in bulk, about 45 minutes.

8. Preheat oven to 350°F. Brush with egg white and sprinkle with almonds. Bake about 30 minutes or until browned.

Makes 1 large coffeecake (15 to 18 servings)

BLUEBERRY-CHEESE PANCAKES

2 cups all-purpose flour
2 teaspoons baking powder
¼ teaspoon baking soda
¼ teaspoon salt
2 tablespoons sugar
2 tablespoons wheat germ
1½ cups milk
1 cup cottage cheese, pressed through a sieve
1 egg, lightly beaten
¼ cup vegetable oil
1 cup fresh or frozen blueberries

1. Sift flour, baking powder, baking soda and salt into medium bowl. Stir in sugar and wheat germ; set aside.

2. Combine milk, cottage cheese, egg and oil in small bowl.

3. Pour liquid ingredients, all at once, into dry; stir until moistened. Add additional milk if batter is too thick; it should pour easily from spoon. Gently stir in blueberries.

4. Preheat griddle or large skillet over medium heat; grease lightly. Pour about ½ cup batter onto hot griddle for each pancake. Cook until tops of pancakes are bubbly and appear dry; turn and cook until lightly browned, about 2 minutes.   *Makes about 10 pancakes*

Keeping Pancakes Warm

You can keep pancakes warm until ready to serve by placing them on a plate or baking dish in a 200°F oven. Layer paper towels between to absorb steam and keep them from getting soggy.

Blueberry-Cheese Pancakes

MUFFIN SURPRISE

These muffins need no butter or jam, that's the surprise inside! They are perfect for a buffet.

1½ cups all-purpose flour
2½ teaspoons baking powder
¼ teaspoon salt
1 cup oat bran
½ cup packed light brown sugar
1 cup milk
⅓ cup vegetable oil
2 eggs, lightly beaten
1 teaspoon vanilla extract
1 package (3 ounces) cream cheese
¾ cup apricot-pineapple jam

1. Preheat oven to 425°F. Grease 12 (2½-inch) muffin cups.

2. Sift flour, baking powder and salt into large bowl. Stir in oat bran and brown sugar; set aside. In small bowl, combine milk, oil, eggs and vanilla. Stir milk mixture into dry ingredients just until moistened.

3. Cut cream cheese into 12 equal pieces. Spoon about ½ of batter into prepared muffin cups, filling about ⅓ full. Spoon about 1 tablespoon jam on top of batter. Top with 1 piece of cream cheese. Spoon remaining batter over jam and cheese, filling each muffin cup ⅔ full. Bake about 14 to 16 minutes or until browned.   *Makes 12 muffins*

Honey Butter

For a sweet spread that is terrific on everything from muffins to toast, combine equal amounts of softened butter or margarine and honey, then add a little vanilla extract. You'll want to keep a batch of this on hand to sweeten all your breakfasts.

Top: Spicy Sweet Potato Muffins (page 72) Bottom: Muffin Surprise

STRAWBERRY &
BANANA STUFFED
FRENCH TOAST

1 loaf (12 inches) French bread
2 tablespoons strawberry jam
4 ounces cream cheese, softened
1/4 cup chopped strawberries
1/4 cup chopped banana
6 eggs, lightly beaten
3/4 cup milk
3 tablespoons butter or margarine, divided
Strawberry Sauce (page 10)

1. Cut French bread into eight 1½-inch slices. Make pocket in each slice by cutting slit from top of bread almost to bottom.

2. Combine jam, cream cheese, strawberries and banana in small bowl to make filling.

3. Place heaping tablespoon of strawberry filling into each pocket. Press back together.

4. Beat eggs and milk in wide shallow bowl. Add bread; let stand to coat, then turn to coat other side.

5. Heat 2 tablespoons butter in large skillet over medium-low heat. Add bread slices; cook until brown. Turn and cook other side. Remove and keep warm. Repeat with remaining butter and bread slices. Serve with Strawberry Sauce.   *Makes 8 slices*

Here is a simple way to tell if the pan is hot enough to cook your eggs, pancakes or French toast. After heating the pan, flick a few drops of water onto it. If the pan is hot enough the water should skitter and dance around before evaporating. If the water does not hop around, continue heating the pan and try again. If the water evaporates immediately, the pan is too hot. Remove it from the heat for a minute or two to cool it off.

Strawberry & Banana Stuffed French Toast with Strawberry Sauce (page 10)

SPICY SWEET POTATO MUFFINS

The unusual addition of sweet potatoes makes this a very moist and tasty muffin.

2 tablespoons packed brown sugar
1 teaspoon ground cinnamon
1½ cups all-purpose flour
2 teaspoons baking powder
1 teaspoon ground cinnamon
½ teaspoon salt
½ teaspoon baking soda
½ teaspoon ground allspice
⅓ cup packed brown sugar
1 cup mashed cooked or canned sweet potatoes
¾ cup buttermilk
¼ cup vegetable oil
1 egg, beaten

1. Preheat oven to 425°F. Grease 12 (2½-inch) muffin cups.

2. Combine 2 tablespoons brown sugar and cinnamon in small bowl; set aside.

3. Sift flour, baking powder, cinnamon, salt, baking soda and allspice into large bowl. Stir in ⅓ cup brown sugar.

4. In medium bowl, combine sweet potato, buttermilk, oil and egg. Stir buttermilk mixture into dry ingredients just until combined. Spoon batter into prepared muffin cups, filling each ⅔ full. Sprinkle each muffin with ½ teaspoon of cinnamon mixture. Bake about 14 to 16 minutes or until toothpick inserted in center comes out clean.   *Makes 12 muffins*

RAISIN OAT SCONES

These scones are also perfect with a cup of afternoon tea.

2 cups all-purpose flour
2 teaspoons baking powder
½ teaspoon baking soda
¼ teaspoon salt
1 cup rolled oats
½ cup butter or margarine, chilled, cut into pieces
1 cup raisins
About 1 cup buttermilk

1. Preheat oven to 425°F. Grease baking sheet.

2. Sift flour, baking powder, baking soda and salt into medium bowl. Stir in oats. Using pastry blender or 2 knives, cut in butter until mixture resembles coarse crumbs. Add raisins. Stir in enough buttermilk to make soft dough.

3. Turn out dough onto lightly floured surface; knead until smooth. Roll out dough to 12 × 10-inch rectangle. Cut into 2-inch squares.

4. Arrange scones on prepared baking sheet. Bake about 15 minutes or until browned.

Makes 30 scones

CARAMEL-TOPPED MEGA MUFFINS

1 cup raisin and bran cereal
3/4 cup milk
1/4 cup unprocessed wheat bran
3/4 cup molasses
1/4 cup vegetable oil
1 egg, beaten
2 cups all-purpose flour
1 tablespoon baking powder
2 teaspoons ground cinnamon
1/2 teaspoon baking soda
1/2 teaspoon salt
1/2 cup raisins (optional)
3 tablespoons butter or margarine
3 tablespoons packed brown sugar
2 tablespoons light corn syrup

1. Preheat oven to 350°F. Grease 6 large (4-inch) muffin cups.

2. Combine cereal, milk and wheat bran in medium bowl. Let stand about 10 minutes to soften. Stir in molasses, oil and egg. Sift flour, baking powder, cinnamon, baking soda and salt into large bowl. Stir liquid ingredients into dry ingredients just until combined. Stir in raisins.

3. Fill muffin cups, using about 1/2 cup for each muffin. Bake 28 to 30 minutes or until toothpick inserted in center comes out clean. Immediately turn out on cooling rack.

4. Combine butter, brown sugar and corn syrup in small saucepan over medium heat. Cook, stirring constantly, until sugar has dissolved. Bring to a boil. Cook, stirring constantly, 3 to 4 minutes or until thickened. Pour about 1 tablespoon of mixture over each muffin.

Makes 6 large muffins

SPECIAL BRUNCHES

When planning that next special get-together, check out these scrumptious dishes suitable for all kinds of brunches. Everything from crêpes and croissants to hash and ham is included here. You're sure to find one (or more) perfect for the occasion.

Pictured here are Shrimp-Spinach Crêpe Stack and Orange Juice & Champagne; see page 76 for recipes.

SHRIMP-SPINACH CRÊPE STACK

1 recipe Creamed Spinach (page 44)
1 tablespoon vegetable oil
½ medium onion, chopped
1 clove garlic, minced
8 ounces fresh mushrooms, sliced
8 ounces small cooked shrimp
2 tablespoons lemon juice
¼ teaspoon dried leaf tarragon
½ teaspoon salt
⅛ teaspoon freshly ground pepper
6 (6½-inch) Crêpes (page 9)
1 cup (4 ounces) shredded Swiss cheese

1. Prepare Creamed Spinach; set aside.

2. Heat oil in medium skillet over medium heat; add onion and garlic. Cook, stirring occasionally, until onion is tender. Add mushrooms; cook until mushrooms are tender.

3. Continue cooking until moisture has evaporated. Stir in Creamed Spinach, shrimp, lemon juice, tarragon, salt and pepper.

4. Preheat oven to 375°F. Place 1 crêpe in lightly greased shallow baking dish. Spread ¾ cup shrimp filling over crêpe. Repeat layers with remaining crêpes and filling, ending with crêpe. Sprinkle top with cheese. Bake about 30 minutes or until filling is heated through. Cut into wedges to serve. *Makes 4 servings*

Rolled Shrimp-Spinach Crêpes: Use 8 (6½-inch) crêpes. Prepare filling as above. Spoon about ⅓ cup of filling on each crêpe. Roll to enclose filling. Place in lightly greased 13×9-inch baking dish. Repeat with remaining crêpes and filling. Sprinkle with cheese. Bake about 15 minutes or until filling is heated through. *Makes 4 servings*

ORANGE JUICE & CHAMPAGNE

6 teaspoons orange-flavored liqueur
1 quart orange juice, chilled
1 bottle (750 ml) champagne, chilled

Pour 1 teaspoon liqueur into each of 6 wine glasses. Fill each two-thirds full with orange juice. Fill glasses with champagne.

Makes 6 servings

HAM & CHEESE QUESADILLAS

½ cup (2 ounces) shredded Monterey Jack cheese
½ cup (2 ounces) shredded Cheddar cheese
4 (10-inch) flour tortillas
4 ounces ham, finely chopped
¼ cup chopped canned green chilies
Salsa (optional)

1. Combine cheeses; divide equally between 2 tortillas. Place ham and green chilies over cheese. Top each with another tortilla.

2. Heat large skillet over medium heat. Add 1 quesadilla; cook until cheese starts to melt and bottom is browned, about 2 minutes. Turn over and cook other side until browned. Remove and keep warm while cooking remaining quesadilla. Cut each quesadilla into 8 wedges. Serve with salsa, if desired.   *Makes 2 servings*

GREEK THREE PEPPER SALAD

½ cup olive oil
2 tablespoons lemon juice
1 tablespoon water
2 teaspoons white wine vinegar
1 tablespoon chopped fresh parsley
¾ teaspoon minced fresh oregano *or* ¼ teaspoon dried
    leaf oregano
½ teaspoon sugar
1 red bell pepper, thinly sliced
1 green bell pepper, thinly sliced
1 yellow or orange bell pepper, thinly sliced
½ red onion, thinly sliced
½ cup Greek-style olives
2 ounces feta cheese, crumbled
Salt and pepper to taste

1. Pour oil into small bowl. Add lemon juice, water, vinegar, parsley, oregano and sugar; whisk until thickened.

2. Combine peppers, onion and olives in large bowl. Add dressing. Toss to combine, cover and let stand at room temperature 1 hour. Drain off excess dressing. Add cheese to pepper mixture; toss. Season with salt and pepper.   *Makes 6 servings*

CHICKEN WITH MUSHROOM SAUCE

MUSHROOM SAUCE
- 3 tablespoons butter or margarine
- 8 ounces fresh mushrooms, sliced
- 3 tablespoons all-purpose flour
- 1½ cups chicken broth
- 1 tablespoon minced chives
- 1 tablespoon minced parsley
- 1 teaspoon Dijon-style mustard
- ¼ teaspoon salt
- ⅛ teaspoon freshly ground pepper
- ½ cup sour cream

CHICKEN
- 1 tablespoon vegetable oil
- 4 boneless skinless chicken breast halves
- 4 slices ham
- 4 slices Monterey Jack cheese
- 2 English muffins, split and toasted
- ½ red bell pepper, cut into thin strips

1. For Mushroom Sauce, melt butter in medium saucepan over medium heat. Add mushrooms; cook until tender. Remove with slotted spoon; set aside. Stir flour into pan; cook until bubbly. Slowly whisk in broth.

2. Add mushrooms, chives, parsley, mustard, salt and pepper. Cook, stirring constantly, until thickened. Stir in sour cream; heat until hot. *Do not boil.* Keep warm on very low heat.

3. For Chicken, heat oil in large skillet over medium heat. Add chicken; cook, turning occasionally, about 8 minutes or until chicken is browned and no longer pink in center.

4. Reduce heat to low; place ham, then cheese on chicken. Cover and cook 1 to 2 minutes or just until cheese melts. Place chicken on English muffins. Spoon sauce over chicken and top with pepper strips.

Makes 4 servings

A combination of melons (honeydew, watermelon, cantaloupe or any of the regional varieties) cut into different shapes, make a charming accompaniment to many brunch dishes. For a distinctive touch, top each serving with a splash of champagne.

Chicken with Mushroom Sauce

SMOKED SALMON LAVASH

If smoked salmon exceeds your budget, substitute any smoked fish. Lavash (also spelled lavosh or lahvosh) is a thin cracker-bread available in several sizes in supermarkets.

4 ounces cream cheese, softened
1 tablespoon lemon juice
1/4 teaspoon prepared horseradish
4 small (about 5 inch) lavash
4 ounces sliced smoked salmon
1/2 red onion, thinly sliced
2 tablespoons capers, drained

Combine cream cheese, lemon juice and horseradish in small bowl. Spread carefully over lavash. Top with salmon, onion and capers.

Makes 4 servings

ENDIVE-TOMATO SALAD

1/4 cup olive oil
1 tablespoon rice vinegar
1 tablespoon balsamic vinegar or white wine vinegar
1 tablespoon water
2 tomatoes, thinly sliced
2 teaspoons chopped fresh basil *or* 3/4 teaspoon dried leaf basil
2 teaspoons chopped fresh parsley
1 head Belgian endive, separated into leaves

1. To prepare dressing, combine oil, vinegars and water in small bowl. Whisk until thickened; set aside.

2. Arrange tomatoes in center of round platter. Sprinkle with basil and parsley. Tuck endive leaves under tomato slices, arranging like spokes in a wheel. Drizzle dressing over salad.

Makes 4 servings

Smoked Salmon Lavash

HAM-EGG-BRIE STRUDEL

Make two of these for a special brunch.

4 eggs
1 tablespoon minced green onion
1 tablespoon minced parsley
¼ teaspoon salt
⅛ teaspoon freshly ground pepper
1 tablespoon vegetable oil
4 sheets filo pastry
2 tablespoons butter or margarine, melted
3 ounces sliced ham
3 ounces Brie

1. Preheat oven to 375°F.

2. Lightly beat eggs; add onion, parsley, salt and pepper. Heat oil in medium skillet over medium-low heat. Add egg mixture. Cook and stir until softly scrambled. Set aside.

3. Place 1 filo sheet on large piece of waxed paper. Brush lightly with butter. Top with second filo sheet; brush with butter. Repeat with remaining filo. Arrange ½ of ham slices near short end of pastry, leaving 2-inch border around short end and sides. Place scrambled eggs on ham. Cut Brie into small pieces. Place over eggs. Top with remaining ham.

4. Fold long sides of filo in. Fold short end over ham. Use waxed paper to roll pastry to enclose filling. Place on lightly greased baking sheet, seam-side down. Brush with remaining butter. Bake about 15 minutes or until lightly browned.

Makes 4 servings

QUICK APRICOT SYRUP

This super-easy syrup dresses up toaster waffles and French toast but is also great mixed with yogurt or poured over hot cereal.

¾ cup apricot preserves
¾ cup apple juice

Combine preserves and apple juice in medium saucepan over medium heat. Bring to a boil. Cook, stirring occasionally, until slightly thickened. Serve warm over pancakes, waffles or French toast.

Makes about 1 cup

Ham-Egg-Brie Strudel with Endive-Tomato Salad (page 81)

BROCCOLI-SALMON QUICHE

1 (9-inch) Pastry Shell (page 86)
1 tablespoon vegetable oil
1½ cups chopped broccoli
⅓ cup chopped onion
⅓ cup chopped red bell pepper
½ cup (2 ounces) shredded Swiss cheese
1 cup flaked canned or cooked salmon
    (about 5 ounces)
3 eggs, beaten
1¼ cups milk
1 teaspoon dried leaf tarragon
¼ teaspoon salt
⅛ teaspoon freshly ground pepper

1. Preheat oven to 425°F.

2. Place piece of foil inside pastry shell; partially fill with uncooked beans or rice. Bake 10 minutes. Remove foil and beans; continue baking 5 minutes or until lightly browned. Let cool.

3. *Reduce oven temperature to 375°F.*

4. Heat oil in medium skillet over medium heat. Add broccoli, onion and bell pepper; cook and stir 3 to 4 minutes or until crisp-tender. Set aside to cool.

5. Sprinkle cheese over bottom of pastry shell. Arrange salmon and vegetables over cheese.

6. Combine eggs, milk, tarragon, salt and pepper in medium bowl. Pour over salmon and vegetables.

7. Bake 35 to 40 minutes or until filling is puffed and knife inserted in center comes out clean. Let stand 10 minutes before cutting.

Makes 6 servings

Broccoli-Salmon Quiche

Pastry Shell

1½ cups all-purpose flour
¼ teaspoon salt
¼ cup butter or margarine, chilled
¼ cup shortening
4 to 5 tablespoons cold water

1. Combine flour and salt in large bowl. With pastry blender or 2 knives, cut in butter and shortening until mixture resembles cornmeal.

2. Add water, 1 tablespoon at a time; stir just until mixture holds together. Knead lightly with your hands to form ball. Wrap in plastic wrap and refrigerate 30 minutes.

3. Roll out dough on lightly floured surface to 12-inch circle. Gently press into 9-inch quiche dish or pie pan. Trim edges and flute.

PAPAYA-KIWIFRUIT SALAD WITH ORANGE DRESSING

Enjoy the tropical sweet-tart combination of papaya and kiwifruit in this easy-to-make salad.

1 papaya
4 kiwifruit
6 tablespoons frozen orange juice concentrate, thawed
3 tablespoons honey
1 cup sour cream
1 tablespoon grated orange peel
1 tablespoon grated lime peel

1. Peel and remove seeds from papaya. Slice lengthwise into thin slices.

2. Peel kiwifruit and cut crosswise into thin slices. Arrange papaya and kiwifruit on 4 salad plates.

3. Combine orange juice concentrate and honey in small bowl. Stir in sour cream. Spoon dressing over salads; sprinkle with peels.

Makes 4 servings

SAUSAGE & APPLE QUICHE

Shredded apple adds a terrific flavor twist to this fabulous quiche.

1 (9-inch) Pastry Shell (page 86)
½ pound bulk spicy pork sausage
½ cup chopped onion
¾ cup shredded, peeled tart apple
1 tablespoon lemon juice
1 tablespoon sugar
⅛ teaspoon crushed red pepper flakes
1 cup (4 ounces) shredded Cheddar cheese
3 eggs
1½ cups half-and-half
¼ teaspoon salt
Ground black pepper

1. Preheat oven to 425°F.

2. Place piece of foil inside pastry shell; partially fill with uncooked beans or rice. Bake 10 minutes. Remove foil and beans; continue baking pastry 5 minutes or until lightly browned. Let cool.

3. *Reduce oven temperature to 375°F.*

4. Crumble sausage into large skillet; add onion. Cook over medium heat until meat is browned and onion is tender. Spoon off and discard pan drippings.

5. Add apple, lemon juice, sugar and chili pepper to skillet. Cook on medium-high, stirring constantly, 4 minutes or until apple is just tender and all liquid is evaporated. Let cool.

6. Spoon sausage mixture into pastry shell; top with cheese. Whisk eggs, half-and-half, salt and dash of black pepper in medium bowl. Pour over sausage mixture.

7. Bake 35 to 45 minutes or until filling is puffed and knife inserted in center comes out clean. Let stand 10 minutes before cutting.

Makes 6 servings

STRAWBERRY-PEACH COOLER

1 cup sliced strawberries
1 cup chopped peaches
2 tablespoons sugar
1 bottle (750 ml) white wine, chilled
1 bottle (1 quart) sparkling water, chilled
Mint sprigs
Ice

1. Combine strawberries and peaches in small bowl. Sprinkle with sugar; stir gently. Let stand at room temperature 30 minutes.

2. Pour fruit into punch bowl. Gently pour in wine and water. Add mint sprigs and ice. *Makes about 2 quarts*

Non-Alcoholic Cooler: Use only 1 tablespoon sugar. Substitute 1 quart apple juice for wine.

SPARKLING APPLE PUNCH

2 bottles (750ml each) sparkling apple cider, chilled
1½ quarts papaya or apricot nectar, chilled
Ice
1 or 2 papayas, peeled and chopped
Orange slices, quartered

Combine apple cider, papaya nectar and ice in punch bowl. Add papaya and orange slices. *Makes about 4 quarts*

Papaya

Papaya is a tropical fruit with a flavor similar to melon. It is available year-round. You can tell the fruit is ripe when at least half the skin has turned yellow.

Left: Sparkling Apple Punch
Right: Strawberry-Peach Cooler

STEAK HASH

The next time you have steak and baked potatoes, plan on using the leftovers for this easy brunch dish.

2 tablespoons vegetable oil
1 green bell pepper, chopped
1/2 medium onion, chopped
1 pound russet potatoes, baked, chopped
8 ounces cooked steak or roast beef, cut into 1-inch cubes
Salt and freshly ground pepper
1/4 cup (1 ounce) shredded Monterey Jack cheese
4 eggs

1. Heat oil in medium skillet over medium heat. Add bell pepper and onion; cook until tender. Stir in potatoes; reduce heat to low. Cover and cook, stirring occasionally, about 10 minutes or until potatoes are hot.

2. Stir in steak; season with salt and pepper. Sprinkle with cheese. Cover; cook about 5 minutes or until steak is hot and cheese is melted. Spoon onto 4 plates.

3. Prepare eggs as desired; top each serving with 1 egg.

Makes 4 servings

MAPLE-GLAZED HAM

4 slices ham (3 ounces each)
1/4 cup maple syrup
1 teaspoon Dijon-style mustard

1. Preheat broiler.

2. Place ham slices on broiler pan. Combine syrup and mustard in small bowl. Brush each slice with about 1 1/2 teaspoons of syrup mixture.

3. Broil 4 inches below heat about 4 minutes or until ham starts to brown. Turn and brush with remaining syrup mixture. Broil until browned.

Makes 4 servings

Steak Hash

INDEX